I Dream My Brother Plays Baseball

For Kevin

I Dream My Brother Plays Baseball

Lisa L. Siedlarz

CLEMSON UNIVERSITY
DIGITAL PRESS

Works produced at Clemson University by the Center for Electronic and Digital Publishing, including *The South Carolina Review* and its themed series "Virginia Woolf International," may be found at our Web site: http://www.clemson.edu/caah/cedp. Contact the director at 864-656-5399 for information.

CLEMSON UNIVERSITY
DIGITAL PRESS

Published by Clemson University Digital Press at the Center for Electronic and Digital Publishing, Clemson University, Clemson, South Carolina.

Produced with the Adobe Creative Suite CS3 and Microsoft Word. This book is set in Adobe Garamond Pro and was printed by Standard Register Incorporated.

Editorial Assistant: Jordan Mckenzie.

To order copies, contact the Center for Electronic and Digital Publishing, Strode Tower, Box 340522, Clemson University, Clemson, South Carolina 29634-0522. An order form is available at the digital press Web site (see above).

Photo on page 20 by Kevin Siedlarz
Photo of author on page 30 by Joy Bush
Cover art by Keith Demanche at Haunted Milk Design

Contents

Acknowledgments

Grateful acknowledgment is made to the editors of the following journals in which these poems have appeared, sometimes in slightly different versions:

"Afghani Summer," *The MacGuffin*, Winter 2009

"Call to Prayer," *The MacGuffin*, Winter 2009

"Don't Paint in Camels," *Louisiana Literature*, 2008

"Eleven Hours to Hell," *Paddlefish*, 2009

"Enduring Freedom," *War, Literature & Arts*, Spring 2009. Winner, 2006 *John Holmes Poetry Prize*.

"I Dream My Brother Plays Baseball," *Connecticut Review*. Winner, 2007 *Leo Connellan Award*

"Teething," *Paddlefish*, 2009

"What We Don't See," *Main Street Rag*, 2007

"Who is She?," *Noctua*, 2008

"First Night, Watchtower," *Minnetonka Review*, 2009

Special thanks to Vivian Shipley, Brian Clements, Gloria Frym, Cecilia Woloch, Tony Fusco, Shula Chernoff, Pat Mattola, Erik Mortenson, Mary Ann Campbell, Dave Holub, Gwen Jones, Kateri Kosek, Chris Gallagher, and PJ Moretti, whose advice and encouragement are priceless. To Avon Dennis, for wings. To Mike Visaggio for unwavering faith & love. And to all of our troops and their families who sacrifice so much.

Sister speaks

ENDURING FREEDOM
FOR MY BROTHER KEVIN

1. They're sending me to Afghanistan

I clench my hands when you tell me this,
nails leaving slices of harvest moons
in my palms. The urge to vomit hits me.
October 2005 in New England, the first
signs of change through trees,
the raspiness of fallen leaves in your voice
as you ask me to assume power of attorney.
I nod because speech sticks like first frost
on a windowpane. I have six months to practice
saying: *Be safe, little brother.*

2. It's what I signed up for

Time is measured by the swinging pine
of the cuckoo clock, each half-hour strike
sharp as a scythe. Our family sits around
the fireplace after Thanksgiving dinner.
You talk about
            a living will.
I face you but see flames rise and fall.
Heat dries my eyes. I refuse to blink for fear
of missing something. I slide back
to our summers of hide-n-seek, innocence amuck
in backyards like bead mongers at Mardi Gras.
You say:
            Cemetery
I take deep breaths to stop from screaming
how can they keep you beyond your eight years?

I know your answer.

3. A copy of my orders.

Iced fingers climb my spine like an old wooden ladder.
Four days until Christmas but these papers fast-forward me
to Ft. Bragg where you'll train for three months before deployment:
Presidential order of activation not to exceed 545 days.

Tears come easier than breathing. Fingers, tissues,
back of hand try to blot out *Hazardous Combat Pay*
no mention of the:
        dog you had to give away
        lost slot on the fire department waiting list
        no plumbing license after two years of school
Dreams crystallize like ice,
a razor's blade scrapes them to powder.
I cup my hands to keep hope from dripping.

4. January 7ᵗʰ

came faster than an M-16 round.
I stand in New Haven's Armory, an American
flag clenched in my hand. Chills
from the ground, soldiers and civilians
mingle, shift weight from left to right
to left again, try to relieve the discomfort
of goodbye. Buses to Ft. Bragg are due
at 3:00. My hope clings like a bad joke.

5. Training in the field begins

for you at four a.m., ends at *twenty-two hundred.*
Wishing your weekly calls would not drip
with exhaustion, we speak of superficials to avoid
the heart of your 18-month isolation.

Laundry – phone calls- PX. Sleep?

6. To sleep somewhere other than Hell.

Your four-day visit home is a small gift
before deployment. Over dinner, you say
I'll understand the barrack's nickname
when I come to see you off. The family
gathers for a quasi-Thanksgiving wearing
masks that crack like thin ice. Jabs
and bickering, it is what we do best.

7. Departure

Three days ago we were landlocked
at Ft. Bragg. You pointed out training sites
for airborne infantry, identified booms
of the mortars you've been training with
for the last three months. Now in Maryland,
I watch Atlantic waves curl in a rush to Ocean
City's shore. A rip tide cuts horizontal
through white foam before gravity pulls back
water and anything caught in its churn.

Saying goodbye was like wrapping my arms
around these five foot swells
that crest and break where land rises as sharply
as the C-130s carrying you westward to Afghanistan.
The sea heaves wall after wall of water,
carrying sunlight across its curves before folding
in on itself, hiding the sparkle in an undertow.
I sit on this sand without the weight of Kevlar,
not having to choose between

cotton or moisture-wick clothes that melt
to skin from the heat transfer of bullets.
I sit here all day, watch surf pound
shore like the rounds of your M-120s.
I want to sit here for 18 months, hold my breath
between each call and correspondence.
But there is beauty in danger. Angry waves
can jerk out my legs, suck me into a dark place.
Sharks hunt just off these shores.
They are hungry.

I'm G.I. Joe

...my youngest brother would say, jumping and fighting,
plastic men bearing arms for his command. He'd stage
battles, blow them apart, stand them up again.
Halloween, he'd wear camouflage and grease smears
on his face. In high school he found Battle Zone stores,
exchanged blue jeans for fatigues. After graduation,
he enlisted. The army motto: *Be all that you can be.*

82nd Airborne, his jumps with sixty-two pound parachutes,
ninety-two pounds of equipment, earned him wings
and blown out knees. Honorably discharged, he joined
the National Guard, 102nd infantry. How he'd go on
about this mortar or that, different rounds and shells,
how those training targets don't shoot back.

ELEVEN HOURS TO HELL

A PATRIOT IS A CITIZEN TRYING TO WAKE FROM THE BURNT-OUT DREAM OF INNOCENCE.
ADRIENNE RICH *ATLAS OF A DIFFICULT WORLD*

1.

One of my dogs is so stoned on tranquilizers her bladder
lets go all over the velour seats of my car just an hour
into our Connecticut to Ft. Bragg North Carolina drive
to see my brother Kevin. She tries to lift her droopy self,
collapses back into her mess. I'm pissed at the vet.
He said the drugs would take the edge off Bear's
pacing and whining. When I call in, he sounds amused,
says one pill for a 75 pound dog usually has no effect.
Don't worry, he says, *it will wear off in four hours.*

I stop every hour for the dogs to stretch their legs.
Noon, I still have to keep my hand on Bear's back
to steady her, help her back into the car. At least now
she sits for a few minutes, head bobbing and nodding.

Roads lined with black snow, mounds shrinking
with every mile. Shrinking, dirtier until they disappear.
I drive with windows open. Three seasons in one day
is a time warp made more warbled by my destination:
seeing my brother off to war.

2.

My family meets at the hotel. It's 95 degrees.
I take a Xanax to smooth my edges. I can't let
my brother carry my unsteadiness to Afghanistan.
Kevin waits for me to get him from the barracks,
just five minutes away. Twenty minutes later,
guards search my trunk, engine, peer beneath my
chassis with a mirrored rod, give the all clear.

I drive straight past the 82nd Airborne Museum,
B-52 bombers and Black Hawks. Past a picnic area
and pond where the barbeque pit is fireless and grass
unbent. Past ladders that lead to the Slide for Life,
platforms fifty feet high. Past adult sized jungle gyms,
rappelling walls. Past white buildings with black windows,
green lawns and no trees. Past a group of men jogging
the black top where heat lifts in waves. Here I turn
onto row upon row of two-story rectangle buildings
that must have been white once, but remind me of
melting roadside snow.

In a crowd of soldiers hanging around, smoking, my brother
stands out, the "Siedlarz" stance with feet planted a foot apart,
knees kinked like a knob on a tree. He points to the parched
parking lot. I close my windows to keep out the dust.

My family has always practiced not touching. Now rules
are illogical. I throw my arms around my brother, he lifts me
so that my back cracks. Fifteen years younger than me,
there was a time when he used to walk on my back.
We thought it fun when he'd fall and my breath huffed.

He puts me down, notices Bear's droopy eyes and squats to pet her.
When Kevin lived with me, she'd cram his dirty socks in her mouth.
At night, she'd dig at the blankets until he pulled them back to let her in.
Now she leans into him so hard he throws his hand to the ground,
I place mine on his shoulder to keep us steady.

This, he says, *is hell.*

Barracks have torn screens, or no screens. Wooden stairs
are splintered and groan. Inside, concrete floors have cracks
that could hold half dollars upright. Paint curls from the ceiling
signs of water seepage spreads from the corner.
There, says my brother, *is our pet cockroach.* It is nearly
the size of a mouse. One of his bunk-mates chuckles. I close
my eyes only to hear the pop of his combat boot deepen my dread.
I can't bear to see the remains, so I go outside.

My brother tells me these buildings were slated for demolition,
windows and doors removed. Slapped back together
so activated troops had some where to stay before deploying.

3.

Kevin ships out in two days to a place where specialists
look for signs of improvised explosives.
Two nights at Best Western where he can swim, drink beer,
not hear mortars exploding. Poolside, the family gathers.
My three brothers stand their stance by the pool.
Kevin leaps in belly-first, the others cannon-ball
in response. Splash slops over the sides. Bear whines
for Kevin and his water play.
I drink a beer in silence. A toast. A prayer.

U.S. Marines are Trading Gunfire and Artillery Shells with Taliban Militants
June 22, 2008 New Haven Register

So warfare is a pastime, like collecting baseball cards.
In the volatile province of Helmand, soldiers move in
and set up post in an attempt to root out fighters.

In the land of opium, troops exchange with insurgents
who fire rockets and mortars at U. S. positions.
Taliban desperate to hold their million dollar enterprise.

The first photo my brother e-mailed me: He stands
fully dressed in Kevlar and helmet, rifle at the ready
behind him poppies smack their red faces in the breeze.

MEMORIAL DAY

I.

Down the street from where Private
First Class Lenzi used to shoot
baskets, his nephews untangle
a flagpole rope from the branch
of a White Oak tree.

The boys hear dribbling and whoops
a pick up game on the same courts
where Uncle Joe taught them layups,
free throws. Untying the knot taxes
their six and eight year old fingers.

Morning sun is criminally bright.
The boys secure and hoist the flag
over the newly installed plaque
in memory of the twenty year old pfc.

II.

My brother's e-mail tells of a BBQ
just like ours, burgers, dogs, salads.
There was music and wiffle ball.
Yes, he writes, *its one hundred degrees*

dusty as hell, and I played wiffle ball.
They even gave us a special treat
get a load of the picture I've attached.

On screen my brother, red faced
and smiling, holds two lobster tails.
Beside him a whole case on ice,
lined up in rows, a mass grave.

Teething

After he spent a year shoving needles through chest cavities,
binding limbs held together by veins, my brother calls me, panicked,
because his first puppy has a loose tooth, black and hanging by gums.

I've seen his E.R. photos: An Afghani soldier took a sniper
bullet to the anus so he is butterflied. A civilian met an IED,
foot and calf held together by achilles flayed like flank steak.

When my brother comes over, his beagle zooms in to greet
my dogs, her tail a helicopter of happy. I call her over,
she leaps up, slobbers on my hand as I pull back her lip.

I put the pup on my table, use a cotton pad to absorb saliva.
A firm tug rips free the dead bicuspid. I ask my brother if
he wants to keep the tooth. He shakes his head, says it smells.

Brother speaks

First Night, Watchtower

No sleep. Swelter chokes, tricks
my brain with shadows so dense
I press night vision goggles to my eyes
until my arms burn and shake.
Beneath stars, rocks and sand crawl
with camel spiders, beige, hairy,
and multi-fanged. Twice the girth
of a double A battery, one chased me
so I crunched it with my boot.
A lone cricket chirs a death dirge.
Distant dogs fire off intermittent barks.
The ra-ta-tat of an automatic weapon
bounces off the Southern Cross,
orange flashes like blinking eyes,
there, and there.
The mosques calls, a hush settles
like dirt. From up high I watch them
bow to Mecca, give thanks.

TEA WITH ELDERS

Dawn breaks with the stench of shit lagoon
where excrement is dumped. A dust devil
whips by portajohns, hot winds of diesel
and disinfectant. Our Terp calls it a Djinn
of free will that whispers *give in to this evil.*

Today we drive through minefields
dressed in pounds: helmet, seven;
ceramic body armor, twenty two;
load-bearing vest packed with batteries,
bullets and grenades, thirty. We are walking
bombs with elephant grace.

The desert is littered: wrecked tanks,
trucks, silver hulls of Russian fighters.
Mosques and schools are rubble. Stucco
and mudbrick huts huddle between walls.
Our boots whoof up knee-high clouds.

Everything is dust in Ass-Crack-istan.
Children with fly-covered smiles spill
out chanting *kalam.* Pens we hand out
are novelties in the villages.

The village elder greets us with a girl
whose mostly bald head is covered
in oozing sores. We give iodine, gauze.
The elder touches his heart, invites us in.
We peel off our armor and sit on the floor.

He presents Khoshgovar, Iranian cola,
hocks spit into a spotted glass, wipes it on
his robe. Antifreeze jugs are ice buckets.
We raise our glasses. *We want Americans
to stay,* he says through our terp, *if you leave,
we will have more war.*

The old man takes my arm, *How to show
my love?* I take his hand in mine, place mine
on his shoulder, tell him *thank you.*

ATF Love

Anti Taliban Forces are the most macho
fighters we know. And the gayest.
These dudes, who carved up Russians
with bayonets, who ride three men

on a Honda 125 bike while on patrol,
slaughter Al Qaeda with grenades
and AK-47s, then kick back and listen
to love songs while holding hands.

Women are for children, men for love.
We laugh, call them the *Butt-Pirate army.*
In our free time, we hang out at their posts,
play cards and watch Van Damme movies.

At night, these ATFs loiter on their small,
meticulously kept lawn lit by lamps made
from old Soviet bomb casings stuck in
the ground and strung with colorful lights.

Arms draped over shoulders and guns, they
sway to music from a boombox. Sometimes
they hire young teen boys to dance and sing
while bearded men with craggy smiles gaze on.

Back at our fort, we sit on upturned crates,
bullshitting, while the wind hits shit lagoon.

JUNKIE

Soldier and civilian look the same
to a bomb. An EMT back home, here

I volunteer my downtime to work
with wounded, ten or more per event.

I'm quick with a needle. Morphine dims
exposed tibia where blood commingles

with blood on my khaki tee. In a makeshift
hospital, I side-step for crash cart, IV's,

and breathing bags. I can plunge a needle
into intercostal space, *one two three* ribs

down from the clavicle. Pin hole collapses
lung. Flutter valve plugs bullet hole,

blocks air, allows seepage of fluids.
Then there's the exit wound.

Tomorrow I have to take apart my M-4.
Q-tips work well removing sand from barrel.

CAMELS

Habibs keep them like pets. Nasty
split-lipped spitsters, the only thing
they're good for is the hair. Blankets,
clothes, tents, even twine.

They say the milk is good for us, sickly
sweet watery, I'd rather drink black coffee.
Even the meat is tough and stringy.
Dung? Burn it for fuel.

I've watched a bull-calf follow this boy
for three days. An average life-span of forty
years, it's likely they'll be buried together.
Ata Allah, they say, gifts from God.

AFGHANI SUMMER

To step off this transport plane in Bagram,
three hours flight from desert to mountain base,
to feel ten degrees fahrenheit smack my face
is like an iced Coors Lite after quitting time
on a Friday, state-side in New Haven.

Each crunch of my boot is a snow-step further
away from that sand-filled forced-air-furnace
where wounded Afghans stagger through dust
storms, clicking their tongues to call for help,
choked by sand eight years removed from rain.

In that desert base, sand fell from my crotch
every time I went to the can. In July it reached
one hundred and sixty degrees three days in a row.
December, and we still wear gloves to hold our
weapons. I hate the heat.

Even camels stand still, move only to turn over
the dirt for its coolness. But rain did come.
Two days steady. Nothing continues to bloom.

LEAVE

Home for Christmas. Unseasonably
seventy degrees and windows wide
on the day of Sgt. Phanuef's funeral
as if Afghanistan came back
with his gathered limbs.

In Connecticut winters, snow often
changes to freezing rain – beautiful
as the snakish road to Mehtar Lam
lined with greeneries and rocky outcrops
perfect for IEDs and an ambush cover.

Snow plows burst through calm
the way a Casualty Notification Officer
erupted Phaneuf's wife and kids,
two weeks before Christmas
when her blue star turned gold.

Driving northeast toward Phaneuf's
funeral, I think of his family,
and mine. I turn around,
go back to my final days at home.

Don't Paint In Camels

Amazing creatures, really. The color of
heaped dunes, scorch just rolls over them.

I've marched their waveless beach, mirages
of smiles disarming and deadly. Those camels

marched knock-kneed and steady. Even under fire
they did not flinch. The mind is treacherous.

I see camels in stitches of multi-colored coats and falling foliage.
In burning bushes of autumn, red is an exploding oil well,

black clouds, souls of those who will never come home.
I'm fine now. I know I'm home when I hold my paint brush

and canvas, a good bottle of wine. I listen to the ocean's
music, become grounded. I will not drown in the legs

of this merlot. Will capture spray of ocean on rocks,
paint a picture of a life not mine.

Bury me in the sand and I will envy how clouds move on
like breath. Cold doesn't faze me, having walked

through dust-deviling hell where thoughts of winter saved
me from suffocation. Here I sit on this beach, sand

slipping through my open fingers to reunite with kin.
Sand is color-blind. Drinks blood as if it were water.

Pictures speak

WHO IS SHE?

I ask my brother, who is home on leave showing me his
photos, from Afghanistan. She looks three maybe four,
wears an emerald tulle dress. The lace collar, like doilies
my grandmother made, drapes her shoulders and chest.

Her neck is thin as a featherless bird's, tendons and blue
veins stick out from taut skin. Her head challenges
the grace of her neck, so she leans into her father
who stares down at her willing her to breathe. Breathe.

Her black eyes are turned inward, away from the endless
dust, endless echoes of gunshots and explosions.
She was ten, my brother says, *just stopped eating.*
He shakes his head. *Lost her will.* I look into her eyes

see how she turns in and in until she is weightless.
Blossoming into wings, did she rise up with the wind?

CALL TO PRAYER
PHOTO SERIES, FARAH PROVINCE, AFGHANISTAN

Everywhere dirt. Drab, fine grit clouds up
with passing cars, rapid footsteps. Wind
zings it into eyes, ears, so that earth is a lover.
Soil is the base for these beige buildings,
sand, water, bits of shale. Even blood and bone
in these mortared structures.

But here a shock of trees cluster the footpath. Mid-day,
Muezzin cries, worshipers cleanse and enter the Mosque,
archways lined with green palmettes. Blue flora fills
the Arabesque, like heaven's peace, like humble voices,
Allahu Akbar, God is great. Yellow interlaced with peach
and pink buds festoon the aura. At its core, black,
where souls offer themselves in dense light.

Two Men Carry an Afghani into the Aid Station, a Bullet in his Leg

Americans cradle him,
arms under his knees and shoulders,
his draped so casually around their necks,
they could be drinking buddies.

His expression reminds me of the black velvet
clown's, head tilted to the right,
a silver drop suspended
between lower lid and grief.

Even as blood leaves a trail
a smile ghosts his face.
In these times, he still remembers.
No surprise someone snapped his picture.

Insurgent Injured in Rollover
My Brother's Photo Series

He is strapped to the table,
a thick olive belt cinching
white swaddle. Blood leaches
below his knees, but the units'
attention is to his head
obscured by a neck brace.

Six men and a woman circle
with tubes, IVs, needles.
He reaches for my brother's
hand. Kevin clasps back, blue
latex against skin a comfort since
he can't understand a word spoken.

The Afghani's grasp gives way,
my brother rests his hand on the table,
moves to his head to work
a breathing bag, one breath every
five seconds: one-one thousand one.

A medic begins compressions, another
prepares a finger long needle, the first
injection into the I.V., the second,
into his heart. The third medic preps
a defibrillator, presses a paddle
to the chest, the other on bruised ribs.

The man's torso rises, his head a cloud.
A murmur, then a whorl. Numb, confused,
does he know the relief when my brother
hears his heart thrum in the stethoscope,
says, *we got him back?*

Why I Don't Watch *Good Morning America*

With faces as fallen as Lucifer from grace,
morning anchors tell us one of their own
field reporters has been wounded by an IED.
They show stock clips of this reporter's
coverage of peace talks, bombings, deaths.

2.2 deaths a day. A scroll bar for the number
wounded by roadside bombs, full coverage
only when friendly fire causes death,
or a soldier empties his clip into civilians
because his buddy was snipered.

Boys come home with hostile fire
looped in their minds. News clips gloss over
second and third tours, ignoring families
widowed to this label of freedom.
Wounded, 25,000 and rising. Short memories

for fractured families. My brother's sergeant
comes home to his wife and kids in a flag draped
coffin. TV doesn't tells how shrapnel severed
him in two. How dangerous reporters' jobs are
covering fire fights.

What We Don't See
A soldier's homecoming, a story on NPR

She must announce herself to him before
walking into a room must close doors so
there is not even the tiniest trigger click
it took just one
can of soup
hitting the table
for her husband
to hurl himself
to the floor as
if about to die

I Dream My Brother Plays Baseball

On the field your platoon strategizes while Afghani
wind blows sand faster than Nolan Ryan's fastball,
blurring vision like rosin in a pitcher's eye. It sticks,
stings as bad as the last time I saw you at Ft Bragg,
a send-off for your twelve month mission.

From the stands I squint to see you as if I'd left my
glasses home. Bases and mound surrounded by dirt,
rocks, I turn and turn in this grey and translucent
gathering of blurred faces & monochromatic baseball
caps ~ *Do you see my brother? Can you see him?*

The crowd jumps up and roars as a soldier rips
a line drive through the gap, slides head first
into second just beneath the tag. A mailman
whose USPS eagle decorates his shoulders
like your army stripes, chases the play, throws

up his right arm to indicate safe. Under his left arm
he carries the package I sent to you a month ago,
labeled: If undeliverable, return to sender.
I take the box from him, hoping to hand-deliver
sunscreen, foot powder, Crystal Lite on the Go.

With my arms full, I run bases calling your name.
Rounding third, white-faced hornets block the way
home, the nest hidden in surrounding caves.

A Note on the Poet

A Note on the Poet

Lisa L. Siedlarz received her Masters in Fine Arts from Western Connecticut State University. She is Editor of *Connecticut River Review* and Managing Editor for *Connecticut Review*. She has won the *John Holmes Poetry Prize* and *Leo Connellan Award* and was nominated for the 2009 Best New Poets Award. She also facilitated a 16 week writing workshop with Vietnam veterans and edited a collection of their work called *The Season of Now*. Lisa Siedlarz works for Southern Connecticut State University and lives in New Haven, Connecticut.